Diet recommendations for TCM - Liver - Fire

Please check these recommendations always with a TCM nutrition consultant, therapist, doctor or dietician. The recipes and the list of ingredients are supporting also the conventional medical therapy. The calorie disclosures of fresh ingredients (fruit and vegetables) vary according to quality and time of harvest. The contents were checked by a dietician and a nutrition consultant for the Traditional Chinese Medicine (TCM).

Author:
©2017 Josef Miligui
www.ebns.at

AF285239

Source:
The lists are created from the EBNS database for nutritional counseling. The database is used by dietitians, therapists and doctors for advising the patient / client.

Literature:
The specialist literature and the training documents of the German and Austrian dietary and traditional Chinese medicine serve as a knowledge base. We have used the documents as a basis of knowledge, adapted it to our experience and completed them.
http://di-book.com

Title Photo:
©2008 Erika Weixlbaumer

Production and publishing:
BoD – Books on Demand, Norderstedt
ISBN: 9783752861488

Diet recommendations for TCM - Liver - Fire

1 Treatment strategy 4
2 Avoid 4
3 Breakfast 4
4 Lunch 4
5 Dinner...5
6 Any time 6
7 Recipes 7
   7.1   8 treasures of rice 7
   7.2   Asparagus with lemon pesto...7
   7.3   Barley mash with steamed pear 8
   7.4   Basic recipe for a beef broth (clear).....................................9
   7.5   Basic recipe for a chicken broth worming............................10
   7.6   Basic recipe for a duck broth 10
   7.7   Basic recipe for a fish broth 11
   7.8   Basic recipe for a reissue soup (Congee) 12
   7.9   Basic recipe for a vegetable soup, nutritious.......................12
   7.10   Basmati rice + Zucchini tofu dish..13
   7.11   Beet salad with salad cucumber..14
   7.12   Black beans with avocado...15
   7.13   Celery and tomato salad 15
   7.14   Celery juice...16
   7.15   Celery salad with lemon and olive oil...................................17
   7.16   Chicken soup with angelica root and buckthorn fruit..........17
   7.17   Compote from rhubarb..18
   7.18   Cooling rice dish with grapefruit 18
   7.19   Cucumber soup 19
   7.20   Fried asparagus with rocket..19
   7.21   Grape juice with hot water...20
   7.22   Italian champignon rice 20
   7.23   Pear compote 21
   7.24   Pear juice 21
   7.25   Potato with dandelion salad 22
   7.26   Raw celery salad 22
   7.27   Rice porridge with shrubs (seeds) Yi Yi Ren.....................23
   7.28   Rice with parsnips...23
   7.29   Roasted millet with Celery sticks...24
   7.30   Salmon on tomato-spinach 24
   7.31   Spinach with Tahini..25
   7.32   Summer Salad..26

7.33   Tae from Dandelionroots.................................27
7.34   Tea from celery sticks....................................27
7.35   Tea from elderberry blossom tea....................27
7.36   Tea from lavender blossoms..........................28
7.37   Tea from mallow...28
7.38   Tea from Melissa..28
7.39   Tea from sage..29
7.40   Tea Green tea..29
7.41   Tea mixture against bile ailments...................30
7.42   Wheat fresh grain porridge with pears............30
8   Effects of food...31
8.1   Use ingredients: recommendable...................31
8.2   Use ingredients: yes.....................................36
8.3   Use ingredients: little...................................37
8.4   Do not use contra-acting foods......................38
9   Herbs and their effects.......................................39
9.1   Basil...39
9.2   Birch leaves..39
9.3   Dill...39
9.4   Dyer's broom herb..39
9.5   Hop...40
9.6   Coriander..40
9.7   Herbs various..40
9.8   Cress..40
9.9   Chives...40
9.10   Lavender blossoms.......................................41
9.11   Lily bulbs...41
9.12   Dandelion (young plants)...............................41
9.13   Balm...41
9.14   Agrimony...42
9.15   Rosemary..42
9.16   Sage..42
9.17   King Solomon's-seal......................................42
9.18   Yam root, yam root tuber...............................43
10 Basics of Nutrition...44
10.1   Nutrition..44
10.2   Recipes...46
10.3   Foodstuffs...46
10.4   Herbs..47
11 Other dietic-books...48

1   Treatment strategy

Cool the fire, calm the liver, lower the fire.
Hot, warm NO (hot and cold), sour LITTLE, everything else YES

2   Avoid

Too fat, too much meat, spicy, alcohol, yang cooking methods (grilling, frying, frying), coffee, sugar, spicy, yogurt tea, garlic, mineral water, sausage, cheese, ham, smoked.

3   Breakfast

kkal. per serving

Barley mash with steamed pear 113
Beet salad with salad cucumber 264
Black beans with avocado 263
Celery juice 33
Compote from rhubarb 48
Cooling rice dish with grapefruit 234
Cucumber soup 95
Fried asparagus with rocket 148
Italian champignon rice 256
Pear compote 100
Pear juice 180
Potato with dandelion salad 162
Raw celery salad 590
Rice porridge with shrubs (seeds) Yi Yi Ren 211
Rice with parsnips 206
Roasted millet with Celery sticks 400
Tea from lavender blossoms 0
Tea from sage 4
Tea Green tea 2
Wheat fresh grain porridge with pears. 309

4   Lunch

8 treasures of rice 212
Asparagus with lemon pesto 171
Barley mash with steamed pear 113
Basmati rice + Zucchini tofu dish 145
Beet salad with salad cucumber 264

Black beans with avocado 263
Celery and tomato salad 245
Celery juice 33
Chicken soup with angelica root and buckthorn fruit 77
Compote from rhubarb 48
Cooling rice dish with grapefruit.. 234
Cucumber soup.. 95
Fried asparagus with rocket 148
Italian champignon rice 256
Pear compote 100
Pear juice... 180
Potato with dandelion salad.. 162
Raw celery salad... 590
Rice porridge with shrubs (seeds) Yi Yi Ren................................. 211
Rice with parsnips 206
Roasted millet with Celery sticks 400
Salmon on tomato-spinach.. 364
Spinach with Tahini 150
Summer Salad 281
Tea from lavender blossoms 0
Tea from sage... 4
Tea Green tea... 2
Wheat fresh grain porridge with pears. 309

5   Dinner

Asparagus with lemon pesto 171
Basmati rice + Zucchini tofu dish... 145
Beet salad with salad cucumber... 264
Black beans with avocado 263
Celery and tomato salad 245
Celery juice 33
Chicken soup with angelica root and buckthorn fruit 77
Compote from rhubarb 48
Cooling rice dish with grapefruit.. 234
Fried asparagus with rocket 148
Pear compote 100
Pear juice... 180
Potato with dandelion salad.. 162
Raw celery salad... 590
Rice porridge with shrubs (seeds) Yi Yi Ren................................. 211
Rice with parsnips 206
Roasted millet with Celery sticks 400

Salmon on tomato-spinach 364
Spinach with Tahini 150
Summer Salad 281
Tea from lavender blossoms 0
Tea from sage 4
Tea Green tea 2
Wheat fresh grain porridge with pears. 309

6   Any time

Celery juice 33
Compote from rhubarb 48
Pear compote 100
Pear juice 180
Potato with dandelion salad 162
Rice porridge with shrubs (seeds) Yi Yi Ren 211
Rice with parsnips 206
Roasted millet with Celery sticks 400
Tea from lavender blossoms 0
Tea from sage 4
Tea Green tea 2
Wheat fresh grain porridge with pears. 309

7 Recipes

(recommendable) = You can use more.
(little) = You should use less than specified or omit.

7.1   8 treasures of rice

Strengthens kidney and bladder, builds up Qi, strengthens the spleen, repels moisture, reduces internal heat, prevents cancer, builds heart, calms nerves.
Cooking time approx. 1 hour
Calories p. portion: 212
4 portions

Quantity of ingredients
Lily bulbs 1 table spoon / 5g. (recommended)..................................*
Longane 1 table spoon / 5g. ()..*
King Solomon's-seal 1 table spoon / 5g. (recommended).................*
Yam root, yam root tuber 1 table spoon / 5g. (recommended)...........*
Coix (seeds) YiYi Ren 1 table spoon / 5g. (recommended) ....*
Rice wild (nature rice) 1 1/2 cups / 240g. (yes) ....metal
Water 8-10 cups / 800g. (yes) .... earth

Cooking instructions:
Each one 1 tbsp: Bai He, Longan, Yu Zhu, Da Zao, Shan Yao, Lian Mi, Yi Yi Ren, Qian Shi
Add hot water and soak for about 30 minutes. Then add 1 - 2 cups of rice (normal) and simmer for 1/2 to 1 hour until the rice is very soft. Or: Cook for about 3 hours with the herbs a congee. Then the herbs do not have to be soaked.

7.2   Asparagus with lemon pesto

Nourishes Yin from lungs and kidney, produces humors, feeds Yin, moisturizes, relaxes, builds up Qi, spreads, cools heat, keeps fluids, reduces internal wind, forces stomach, moisten the lungs and large intestine.
Cooking time approx. 20 min
Calories p. portion: 172
2 portions
Allergens: H

Quantity of ingredients

Asparagus (green or white) 1,1 lbs / 500g. (yes)........................ earth
Lemon 1 piece / 35g. (yes)...wood
Water hot 1/2 cup / 50g. (yes) ....*
Boxhorn clover seeds 1 pinch / 0,2g. ().................................*
Olive oil 2 table spoons / 20g. (recommended) .... earth
Almond 1 table spoon / 8g. (recommended) .... earth
Sugar cane sugar 1 pinch / 0,5g. (little) .... earth
Garlic 1 clove / 2g. ()..metal
Pepper (ground) 1 pinch / 0,2g. (little)......................................metal
Salt 1 pinch / 0,5g. (recommended)...water

Cooking instructions:
Peel the asparagus (the whites whole, the greens only at the bottom). Peel and cut diagonally into pieces about 3 cm long. In the steam sieve the white about 12 minutes, the green about 10 minutes to cook. Cut the lemon into small pieces, remove seeds. Add the remaining ingredients and puree to a creamy sauce. Arrange the asparagus and cover with the lemon pesto.
This fits rice, bulgur or millet.

7.3   Barley mash with steamed pear

Moisturizes lungs, cools heat, reduced hot lung mucus, produces humors, moisturizes, relaxes, builds up Qi, spreads, forces spleen, cools bladder, diuretic, moisturizes intestines, relaxes, builds up Qi, spreads.
Cooking time approx. 25 min
Calories p. portion: 114
5 portions
Allergens: A

Quantity of ingredients

Water 10 cups / 1200g. (yes).. earth
Barley 1 cup / 120g. (yes)... earth
Ginger fresh 2 slices / 2g. (little) ....metal
Cardamom 3 capsules / 1g. (recommended) ....*
Salt 1 pinch / 1g. (recommended)..water
Pear 1 piece / 200g. (recommended)... earth
Sugar cane sugar 1/2 teaspoon / 5g. (little) .... earth

Cooking instructions:
Grind coarse the barley and roast it dry. Add hot water, add ginger and cardamom and let it swell to a pulp in low heat. Peel and dice the pear and boil for 10 minutes with a little water. At the end, add the stewed pear, a little butter and sweetener.

Variant: If you want to go fast, you can use barley flakes instead of shot.

7.4   Basic recipe for a beef broth (clear)

Strengthens Qi and Yang, is very warming.
Cooking time approx. 4-8 hours
Calories p. portion: 114
10 portions
Allergens: O

Quantity of ingredients

Beef soup meat 1,1 lbs / 500g. .... earth
Beef meatbones 5/8 oz / 200g. .... earth
Vinegar (Red wine vinegar) 1 dash / 3g. .... wood
Juniper berry 8 pieces / 6g. .... fire
Rosemary 1 pinch / 1g. .... fire
Carrot 3 pieces / 210g. .... earth
Parsnip 2 pieces / 300g. .... fire
Leek 1 piece / 200g. .... metal
Ginger fresh 1/2 teaspoon / 5g. .... metal
Lovage 1 stem / 15g. .... metal
Clove 2 pieces / 2g. .... metal
Pimento 6 pieces / 12g. .... metal
Anise (Common Fennel) 2 pieces / 1g. .... earth
Salt 1 teaspoon / 5g. .... water
Water 3,3 lbs / 1300g. .... earth

Cooking instructions:
Heat water, a dash of red wine vinegar, some juniper berries, a little rosemary, bones and meat till it boils; add carrot, parsnip, leek, ginger, lovage, clove, allspice, star anise and a little salt; simmer for 4-8 hours then strain.
Refrigerate for later use.

7.5   Basic recipe for a chicken broth worming

Strengthens Qi and blood, is very warm.
Cooking time approx. 2-3 hours
Calories p. portion: 90
9 portions
Allergens: L

Quantity of ingredients
Chicken meat 1/2 piece / 600g. ....wood
Carrot 2 pieces / 150g. .... earth
Leek 1 stick / 45g. ....metal
Celery root 1 piece / 500g. .... earth
Ginger fresh 2 slices / 2g. ....metal
Fenugreek (Trigonella foenum-graecum) 1 teaspoon / 2g. ....*
Juniper berry 1 teaspoon / 3g. .... fire
Bay leaf 3 pieces / 2g. ....*
Water 4 cup / 900g. .... earth

Cooking instructions:
Remove chicken parts from fat. Place chicken pieces in a saucepan
with hot water and heat till it boils briefly, skimming any resulting foam.
Add coarsely chopped vegetables and all spices and cook over medium
heat for 2 to 3 hours. Strain the finished soup. Throw away vegetables
and bones.
Tip: If you want to use the meat as a soup insert, take out after 45
minutes and return only the bones in the soup.
Refrigerate for later use.

7.6   Basic recipe for a duck broth

Forces Qi, strengthens blood and fluids, nourishes Yin, forces stomach,
cools heat, strengthens spleen and liver.
Cooking time approx. 2-3 hours
Calories p. portion: 61
6 portions
Allergens: L

Quantity of ingredients
Duck (heart) 5/8 oz / 200g. ....wood
Water 2 cup / 450g. .... earth
Duck (slaughtered) 1/4 lbs - 4oz / 100g. ....wood
Carrot 2 pieces / 100g. .... earth
Celery root 1/2 piece / 600g. .... earth

Cooking instructions:
Cook duck pieces with vegetables for 2-3 hours. Sift broth through a fine sieve and refrigerate for later use.

The innards can be reused: You cut them finely and leaves them for a few minutes with fresh vegetables in the broth draw. Sprinkle with parsley before serving.

7.7   Basic recipe for a fish broth

Strengthens kidney Qi and Yin, strengthens blood and fluids, promotes urination.
Cooking time approx. 40 min
Calories p. portion: 128
5 portions
Allergens: DLO

Quantity of ingredients
Fish pieces mixed (fresh water) 3/4 lbs / 300g. ....water
Celery root 1/4 lbs - 4oz / 120g. .... earth
Leek 2 inches / 10g. ....metal
Carrot 2 pieces / 150g. .... earth
White wine 1/2 cup / 125g. ....wood
Lemon 1/2 piece / 50g. ....wood
Bay leaf 2 leaves / 2g. ....*
Peppercorns 3 pieces / 2g. ....metal
Olive oil 1 table spoon / 10g. .... earth
Water 2 cup / 450g. .... earth

Cooking instructions:
Fry celery, chopped carrots and leeks in olive oil, add bay leaf and peppercorns, add pieces of fish and sauté briefly. Add water, add little white wine or lemon. Simmer gently for 30 minutes. Skim off the resulting foam several times. In the end, sift the ingredients through a cloth.
Refrigerate for later use.

7.8 Basic recipe for a reissue soup (Congee)

Warms the stomach and spleen, harmonizes the intestine, forces Qi, reduces moisture.
Cooking time approx. 2-4 hours
Calories p. portion: 140
3 portions
Allergens:

Quantity of ingredients
Rice variety any 1 cup / 120g. ....metal
Water 6 cups / 700g. .... earth

Cooking instructions:
Cook rice and water in a ratio of about 1: 6. The amount of water determines the thickness of the mash (matter of taste).
Put the rice in a saucepan with a heavy lid. It is important to simmer the rice after a short boil on the slightest flame, otherwise it burns.
Boil the rice for 2-4 hours. The longer he cooks, the more he strengthens.
If you want to eat the dish for breakfast, you can put the rice on just before bedtime.
To be on the safe side, you should first check the behavior of your pot and cooker under observation for a similar amount of time, so that nothing burns.
Refrigerate for later use.

7.9 Basic recipe for a vegetable soup, nutritious

Strengthens spleen and lung, regulates Qi flow, builds up Qi, dries out, passes downwardly, strengthens stomach Qi.
Cooking time approx. 2-3 hours
Calories p. portion: 48
5 portions
Allergens: L

Quantity of ingredients
Olive oil 1 table spoon / 4g. .... earth
Onion white 1 piece / 60g. ....metal
Carrot 3 pieces / 200g. .... earth
Parsnip 3/8 lbs - 6oz / 150g. .... fire
Celery root 1 cup / 100g. .... earth
Ginger fresh 1/2 teaspoon / 2g. ....metal

Lemon 1/2 piece / 25g. ....wood
Juniper berry 6 pieces / 6g. .... fire
Thyme dried 1 pinch / 1g. ....metal
Lovage 1 table spoon / 3g. ....metal
Bay leaf 2 leaves / 1g. ....*
Salt 1 pinch / 1g. ....water
Water 3 cups / 650g. .... earth

Cooking instructions:
Cut the vegetables into cubes.
Heat oil in hot pot, fry shortly onions and vegetables.
Add cold water, then add ginger, bay leaf and lemon juice.
Season with juniper, thyme and lovage. Cover for 2 - 3 hours on a low heat and simmer.
The used vegetables should be thrown away.
The basic recipe serves as a soup base and to refine vegetables, legumes or cereals.
If you want to eat vegetable soup immediately, add the desired vegetables half an hour before.
Refrigerate for later use.

7.10 Basmati rice + Zucchini tofu dish

Converts mucus, reduces heat, builds up Qi, nourishes fluids, harmonizes spleen and stomach, forces Lungen Qi.
Cooking time approx. 20 min
Calories p. portion: 146
4 portions
Allergens: E

Quantity of ingredients
Soy Tofu 5/8 lbs - 8oz / 250g. (recommended) .... earth
Olive oil 2 table spoons / 6g. (recommended)............................ earth
Coriander 1/2 teaspoon / 4g. (little)....................................metal
Ginger fresh 1/2 teaspoon / 4g. (little)................................metal
Rice Basmati 1/2 cup / 60g. (recommended) ....metal
Water 3 cups / 200g. (yes) .... earth
Zucchini 1 piece / 700g. (recommended)................................. earth

Cooking instructions:
Cut tofu cubes and marinate with olive oil, tamari, crushed coriander and ginger. Leave at least 1 hour.

Cook Basmati rice with the water. You can season with onion and cardamom.
Roast zucchini and tofu in pan in the hot oil for approx. 5-7 min.
Serve rice and tofu on a plate.
Add the parsley.

Can also be used as a salad for the home and on the go.

7.11 Beet salad with salad cucumber

Nourishing and slightly refreshing, builds up Qi, strengthens blood and fluids, cools and moisturizes, diuretic, reduces damp heat, regulates Qi.
Cooking time approx. 45 min
Calories p. portion: 264
2 portions
Allergens: GMO

Quantity of ingredients
Red beet 4 pieces / 200g. (recommended)................................ earth
Cucumber 1 piece / 250g. (recommended)................................ earth
Olive oil 4 table spoons / 40g. (recommended)......................... earth
Sugar cane sugar 1 pinch / 1g. (little) .... earth
Pepper (ground) 1 pinch / 0,2g. (little)....................................metal
Mustard seeds 1 pinch of powder / 0,2g. (recommended)................*
Dill 1/2 teaspoon (chopped) / 2g. (little) ....metal
Onion (spring onion) 2 pieces / 40g. (little)..............................metal
Salt 1 pinch / 0,5g. (recommended)...water
Vinegar (Apple vinegar) 1 dash / 1g. () ....wood
Sour cream 15% fat 2 table spoons / 20g. (little)............................*
Pepper powder (hot) 1 pinch / 0,3g. (recommended) .... fire

Cooking instructions:
Softly boil beetroot, peel and dice; Peel and dice the cucumber.
Dressing: olive oil, a little whole cane sugar, pepper, mustard powder, dill, finely chopped spring onion, salt, vinegar, a little sour cream and a pinch of rose paprika; stir; mix with the beetroot and let it rest; Add the cucumbers just before serving to keep their light color.
Serve with: millet, which together with the salad makes a simple, light meal.

7.12 Black beans with avocado

Nourishing and slightly refreshing, builds up fluids, filling, nourishes Yin von liver, lungs and colon, moisturizes, relaxes, builds up Qi, spreads, forces stomach and kidney.
Cooking time approx. 1 hour
Calories p. portion: 264
3 portions
Allergens: EN

Quantity of ingredients
Black beans 1 cup / 100g. (recommended)...............................water
Water 4 cups / 450g. (yes) .... earth
Lemon 1 dash / 1g. (yes)..wood
Boxhorn clover seeds 1 pinch (powder) / 0,2g. ()...........................*
Sesame oil 1 table spoon / 10g. (recommended)....................... earth
Ginger fresh 1 teaspoon / 2g. (little)..metal
Wakame 1 inch / 1g. (recommended)......................................water
Soy sauce 1 dash / 1g. (yes)..water
Avocado 1 piece / 300g. (yes) .... earth

Cooking instructions:
Preparation the day before:
Soak 2 cups of black beans in about 6 cups of cold water for 6-8 hours and then strain.
Put the black beans in 4 cups of fresh cold water; add a dash of lemon juice, some fenugreek seed powder, 1 tablespoon of sesame oil, 1 teaspoon of grated ginger; add a piece of wakame or 1 tbsp of hijiki. Simmer for about 45 minutes; puree with the blender; season with plenty of soy sauce.
In the morning: Peel ½ avocado per serving and cut into small boats; Serve with the warm bean paste.
Note: The black beans can be pre-cooked for 2 - 3 days to be used as breakfast or other meals with little effort.

7.13 Celery and tomato salad

Nourishes liver-Yin, produces humors, brings the liver Qi in motion, cools heat, relaxes, builds up Qi.
Cooking time approx. 10 min
Calories p. portion: 245
1 portions
Allergens: GHL

Quantity of ingredients

Celery sticks 3-4 twigs / 50g. (recommended) .... earth
Tomato 4 pieces / 200g. (recommended) .... wood
Basil 3 leaves (fresh) / 1g. () .... metal
Yogurt (natural, 1.5% fat) 2 table spoons / 30g. (yes) .... fire
Olive oil 1/2 teaspoon / 5g. (recommended) .... earth
Lemon juice 1 table spoon / 10g. (yes) .... wood
Salt 1 pinch / 0,5g. (recommended) .... water
Sugar white 1 pinch / 0,5g. (little) .... earth
Pepper (ground) 1 pinch / 0,2g. (little) .... metal
Hazelnuts 2 table spoons / 20g. (recommended) .... earth

Cooking instructions:

Clean celery, possibly remove threads and cut into fine rings. Wash tomatoes and dice. For the sauce, mix yoghurt with olive oil and lemon juice and season with the spices. Add the prepared tomatoes and celery to the sauce and mix. Finely chop whole hazelnuts or sprinkle ground hazelnuts over the fresh food and serve the salad garnished with basil leaves.

7.14 Celery juice

Strengthens stomach Qi, moisturizes, relaxes, builds up Qi, spreads.
Cooking time approx. 5 min
Calories p. portion: 33
1 portions
Allergens: L

Quantity of ingredients

Celery root 1/2 piece / 200g. (recommended) .... earth
Water 1 cup / 120g. (yes) .... earth
Salt 1 pinch / 0,5g. (recommended) .... water

Cooking instructions:

Peel celeriac and cut into pieces and juice. Mix with water and salt as needed.

7.15 Celery salad with lemon and olive oil

Strengthens stomach Qi, moisturizes, relaxes, builds up Qi.
Cooking time approx. 10 min
Calories p. portion: 402
1 portions
Allergens: L

Quantity of ingredients
Celery root 1/2 piece / 200g. (recommended) .... earth
Lemon juice 1/2 piece / 10g. (yes) .... wood
Olive oil 4 table spoons / 40g. (recommended) .... earth

Cooking instructions:
Peel celeriac and cut into pieces and rub. Serve with the lemon juice
and olive oil.

7.16 Chicken soup with angelica root and buckthorn fruit

Strengthens spleen and nourishes the blood and Yin of the liver, forces
Qi and blood, is very warming.
Cooking time approx. 1 1/2 hours
Calories p. portion: 77
3 portions
Allergens: LO

Quantity of ingredients
Basic recipe for a chicken soup 2 cup / 500g. (recommended) .... *
Angelica root 1/8 oz / 5g. (recommended) .... *
Bocksdorn fruits, goji berry dried 1/8 lbs - 2oz / 50g. .... wood

Cooking instructions:
When you cook chicken broth according to basic recipes add angelica
root and Bocksdorn fruits in the last 40 minutes.

Ingestion: Drink 2-3 cups of broth daily.

7.17 Compote from rhubarb

Cools heat, preserves the fluids, contracts, strengthens middle heater, moisturizes.
Cooking time approx. 15 min
Calories p. portion: 48
1 portions

Quantity of ingredients
Rhubarb 1/4 lbs - 4oz / 100g. (yes)...wood
Water 1 cup / 120g. (yes) .... earth
Honey 1 table spoon / 10g. (yes)... earth

Cooking instructions:
Wash rhubarb and cut small. Boil in the water. Allow to cool a little and add the honey.

7.18 Cooling rice dish with grapefruit

Lowers lung Qi, nourishes fluids, dissolves mucus, dries out, passes downwardly, warms the stomach and spleen, harmonizes the intestine, forces Qi, reduces moisture, strengthens Qi and Kidney Jing, moisturizes, relaxes, builds up Qi, spreads.
Cooking time approx. 20 min
Calories p. portion: 234
4 portions
Allergens: GHO

Quantity of ingredients
Rice round grain 1 cup / 120g. (yes)..metal
Water 5 cups / 600g. (yes) .... earth
Hazelnuts 2 table spoons / 20g. (recommended)...................... earth
Raisins 2 table spoons / 20g. () .... earth
Agave nectar 1 table spoon / 10g. (recommended)..........................*
Salt 1 pinch / 0,2g. (recommended)..water
Almond puree 1 table spoon / 10g. ().. earth
Grapefruit (Pomelo) 1 piece / 200g. (yes) .... fire
Butter organic 2 teaspoons / 20g. (recommended) .... earth

Cooking instructions:
Preparation on the eve: Pour round grain rice into cold water and cook. Soak chopped hazelnuts and raisins in some hot water overnight.

In the morning: Stir in a little hot water some agave syrup; add the rice and heat; add a small pinch of salt, almond paste, chopped grapefruit, the soaked chopped hazelnuts and raisins and mix; Serve with a small piece of butter.

7.19 Cucumber soup

Cools and moisturizes, diuretic, reduces damp heat, detoxifies, relaxes, builds up Qi, spreads, distributes mucus, passes downwardly, activates Wei Qi, forces Qi.
Cooking time approx. 20 min
Calories p. portion: 96
4 portions
Allergens: M

Quantity of ingredients
Olive oil 2 table spoons / 35g. (recommended) .... earth
Cucumber 2 pieces / 400g. (recommended) .... earth
Water 2 cup / 500g. (yes) .... earth
Sage 3 leaves / 3g. (recommended) .... fire
Mustard 1/2 teaspoon / 0,5g. (recommended) ....metal
Coriander 1 pinch / 1g. (little) ....metal
Cardamom 1 pinch / 1g. (recommended) .... *
Salt 1 pinch / 1g. (recommended) ....water

Cooking instructions:
Heat oil and roast short the small cucumbers. Add Mustard seeds, coriander, cardamom and salt. Add water. Simmer for 10-15 min. Puree and decorate with fresh chopped sage.

7.20 Fried asparagus with rocket

Nourishes Yin of lungs and kidney, feeds Yin, builds up Qi, forces Qi, strengthens spleen, guides damp heat down.
Cooking time approx. 15 min
Calories p. portion: 149
3 portions
Allergens: G

Quantity of ingredients

Butter organic 1 table spoon / 20g. (recommended).................. earth
Asparagus (green or white) 1,1 lbs / 500g. (yes)........................ earth
Pepper (ground) 1 pinch / 0,5g. (little)....................................metal
Salt 1 pinch / 1g. (recommended)...water
Lemon 1/4 piece / 12g. (yes)..wood
Rucola 2 handful / 30g. (recommended)...................................... fire
Potato 3/4 lbs / 300g. (recommended)...................................... earth

Cooking instructions:
Melt a piece of butter in a hot pan; cut the peeled asparagus into pieces of 3 to 4 cm, fry for about 10 minutes until tender, but crisp. Sprinkle with freshly ground pepper, salt, add a few drops of lemon juice or finely grated lemon zest, finely shredded rucola leaves.
Cook the potatoes in plenty of salted water, then peel.

7.21 Grape juice with hot water

Cooking time approx. 5 min
Calories p. portion: 44
2 portions

Quantity of ingredients

Grape juice red 1 cup / 120g. (recommended).......................... earth
Water 1 cup / 120g. (yes)... earth

Cooking instructions:
Add grape juice to hot water.

7.22 Italian champignon rice

Nourishes blood, moisturizes, relaxes, builds up Qi, spreads, warms the stomach and spleen, harmonizes the intestine, forces Qi, reduces moisture, directs upwards, moisturizes, relaxes, builds up Qi, spreads.
Cooking time approx. 25 min
Calories p. portion: 256
4 portions
Allergens: G

Quantity of ingredients

Rice round grain 1 1/2 cups / 240g. (yes) ....metal
Water 2 cup / 450g. (yes)... earth
Pepper (ground) 1 pinch / 0,2g. (little).....................................metal
Salt 1 pinch / 0,5g. (recommended)...water

Lemon juice 1 dash / 2g. (yes)..wood
Pepper powder (hot) 1 pinch / 0,2g. (recommended) ....fire
Champignon 5/8 lbs - 8oz / 250g. (recommended).................... earth
Olive oil 1 teaspoon / 3g. (recommended) .... earth
Chives 1 teaspoon / 5g. (little) ....metal
Parmesan 2 table spoons / 20g. (little)..................................... earth

Cooking instructions:
Put the round grain rice in cold water 1:6 and cook.
Add ground pepper, salt, plenty of lemon juice, rose paprika, a little olive oil or butter and mix well.
Carefully add in mushrooms, chives or the green parts of the spring onion, and carefully add in some grated Parmesan cheese.
Goes well with vegetables and tofu dishes, tomato sauce dishes.

7.23 Pear compote

Moisturizes lungs, reduces lung mucus, nourishes lungs Qi.
Cooking time approx. 20 min
Calories p. portion: 100
3 portions

Quantity of ingredients
Water 1 1/2 cups / 240g. (yes)... earth
Pear 4 / 500g. (recommended)... earth

Cooking instructions:
Halve organic pears. Cores and skin can be used. Pear in the pot and add water. Simmer for up to 20 minutes until pears are tender.

7.24 Pear juice

Moisturizes lungs, reduces lung mucus, nourishes lungs Qi.
Cooking time approx. 5 min
Calories p. portion: 180
2 portions

Quantity of ingredients
Pear 3 pieces / 600g. (recommended)...................................... earth

Cooking instructions:
Peel pears thinly (vitamins under the skin) and core. Juice in the juicer.

7.25 Potato with dandelion salad

Forces Qi, forces spleen, relieves inflammation, moisturizes, relaxes, builds up Qi, cools liver fire, reduces internal heat, softens knots, dissolves stagnation, passes downwardly, nourishes fluids und Jing, builds up Qi, spreads.
Cooking time approx. 25 min
Calories p. portion: 162
2 portions

Quantity of ingredients
Potato 5/8 lbs - 8oz / 250g. (recommended) .... earth
Onion white 1/2 piece / 20g. (little)..metal
Sunflower oil 1 table spoon / 10g. (recommended) .... earth
Dandelion (young plants) 1/4 lbs - 4oz / 125g. (recommended)..... fire
Salt 1 pinch / 1g. (recommended)...water
Pepper white (ground) 1 pinch / 0,5g. (little)..............................metal

Cooking instructions:
Cook the potatoes in salted water and cut into thin slices. Finely chop the onion. Now season the potatoes with oil, salt and pepper and add the dandelion and mix.

7.26 Raw celery salad

Strengthens stomach Qi, moisturizes, relaxes, builds up Qi, spreads, cools heat, nourishes fluids, keeps fluids, reduces internal wind, forces stomach, forces Qi, forces liver and kidney.
Cooking time approx. 15 min
Calories p. portion: 590
1 portions
Allergens: HLN

Quantity of ingredients
Celery root 1/4 piece / 125g. (recommended) .... earth
Celery sticks 2 branches / 30g. (recommended) .... earth
Sesame oil 4 table spoons / 40g. (recommended) .... earth
Almond puree 2 table spoons / 20g. () .... earth
Pepper (ground) 1 pinch / 0,5g. (little)......................................metal
Salt 1 pinch / 1g. (recommended)...water
Lemon 1/2 cup / 50g. (yes)...wood
Orange juice 1/2 cup / 60g. (yes)...wood
Peppers powder 1 pinch / 1g. (recommended) ....*

Cooking instructions:
Finely grate the celeriac; cut the celeriac into small pieces; celery leaves, cut into small pieces, blanch and combine everything. Dressing: sesame oil, almond paste, pepper, salt, lemon and fresh orange juice, stir well some rose paprika; mix with the celery and let it pass through.

7.27 Rice porridge with shrubs (seeds) Yi Yi Ren

Warms stomach, harmonizes the intestine, forces Qi, reduces moisture, forces spleen, nourishes and forces Lunge, reduces internal heat, moves Qi and blood, diuretic, cools in internal heat.
Cooking time approx. 25 min
Calories p. portion: 212
2 portions

Quantity of ingredients
Water 4 cups / 450g. (yes) .... earth
Rice variety any 1 cup / 120g. (yes)..metal
Lemon peel 1/4 piece / 2g. (yes)... fire
Coix (seeds) YiYi Ren 1/2 cup / 50g. (recommended)......................*
Cress 1 table spoon / 6g. (yes)..metal

Cooking instructions:
Cook rice porridge according to basic recipe with a half cup of Yi Yi Ren and lemon peel. Simmer for 1 hour and then sprinkle cress over it.

7.28 Rice with parsnips

Regulates Qi, dries out, passes downwardly, warms the stomach and spleen, harmonizes the intestine, forces Qi, reduces moisture. moisturizes, relaxes, builds up Qi, spreads. distributes mucus, activates Wei Qi, forces Qi.
Cooking time approx. 45 min
Calories p. portion: 206
3 portions

Quantity of ingredients
Rice variety any 1 cup / 120g. (yes)..metal
Water 1 1/2 cups / 200g. (yes).. earth
Salt 1 pinch / 1g. (recommended)..water
Parsnip 3-4 pieces / 450g. (recommended) .... fire
Olive oil 1 table spoon / 10g. (recommended)............................ earth
Sage 1 teaspoon / 3g. (recommended)... fire

Cooking instructions:
Peel the parsnips and cut into slices. Fry for a short time in oil. Add the rice and fry again for a short time. Add the water and cook it at least 30 min. Sprinkle with fresh chopped sage.

7.29 Roasted millet with Celery sticks

Strengthens spleen and kidney, diuretic, brings the liver Qi in motion, cools heat, moisturizes, relaxes, builds up Qi, spreads.
Cooking time approx. 30 min
Calories p. portion: 400
2 portions
Allergens: L

Quantity of ingredients
Millet 1 cup / 120g. (recommended)... earth
Water 1 1/2 cups / 240g. (yes)... earth
Celery sticks 2 rods / 50g. (recommended).............................. earth
Water 2 table spoons / 30g. (yes).. earth
Herbs various 1 table spoon / 10g. (recommended)........................*
Salt 1 pinch / 1g. (recommended)..water
Sage 3-4 leaves / 2g. (recommended).. fire
Cress 1 teaspoon / 3g. (yes)..metal

Cooking instructions:
Roast millet briefly, pour over water, heat till it boils and let stand for 20 min. to swell.

Cut celery into small pieces and mix with water, salt and fresh herbs and cook for 10 min. Add to the millet. Sprinkle fresh sage or watercress over it.

7.30 Salmon on tomato-spinach

Nourishes blood and Yin, forces Zang-organs, forces stomach and intestines, harmonizes Qi, forces Qi and blood, softens, passes downwardly, forces Qi, forces spleen, relieves inflammation, moisturizes, relaxes, builds up Qi, spreads.
Cooking time approx. 1 hour
Calories p. portion: 365
6 portions
Allergens: D

Quantity of ingredients

Potato 1,1 lbs / 500g. (recommended)..................................... earth
Salt 1 pinch / 1g. (recommended)...water
Salmon 1,3 lbs / 600g. (recommended).................................... water
Rapeseed oil 2 teaspoons / 24g. (recommended)...................... earth
Tomato 1/4 lbs - 4oz / 100g. (recommended) .... wood
Spinach 1,5 lbs / 700g. (yes).. earth
Salt 1 pinch / 1g. (recommended)...water
Pine nuts 4 table spoons / 40g. (recommended)....................... earth
Leek 1/4 lbs - 4oz / 120g. (little)...metal
Olive oil 4 table spoons / 40g. (recommended).......................... earth
Salt 1 pinch / 1g. (recommended)...water
Pepper white (ground) 1 pinch / 0,5g. (little)..............................metal

Cooking instructions:

Peel the potato and cut into cubes, cook in salted water.

Cut the salmon into portions and fry slowly and evenly in a frying pan from both sides, seasoned with salt and pepper, then add the pine nuts and lightly roast.

Blanch spinach in salted water.

Lightly sweat the finely chopped leek with a little rapeseed oil, add the blanched spinach and heat evenly.

Just before serving, add the halved cocktail tomatoes to the spinach and season the vegetables well with salt and pepper.

Arrange the spinach and leek tomato bed with the potatoes, add the salmon and sprinkle with the salted pine nuts.

Drizzle with a little olive oil and serve the dish.

7.31 Spinach with Tahini

Nourishes blood and Yin, forces Zang-organs, forces stomach and intestines, harmonizes Qi, moisturizes lungs, forces Qi, forces spleen, relieves inflammation, moisturizes, relaxes, builds up Qi, spreads, nourishes blood.

Cooking time approx. 20 min
Calories p. portion: 150
4 portions
Allergens: N

Quantity of ingredients
Potato 1,1 lbs / 500g. (recommended).................................... earth
Salt 1 pinch / 0,2g. (recommended)...water
Water 1 cup / 25g. (yes).. earth
Spinach 2,2 lbs / 800g. (yes)... earth
Sesame paste (Tahini) 2 table spoons / 20g. (yes) .... earth

Cooking instructions:
Cook potatoes and peel. Heat water. Blanch spinach. Shake off water
and let it dry and stir with sesame.

7.32 Summer Salad

Nourishes liver-Yin, cools heat, dissolves mucus, forces Xu-conditions,
passes downwardly, brings blood into motion.
Cooking time approx. 10 min
Calories p. portion: 281
1 portions
Allergens: GMNO

Quantity of ingredients
Rucola Handful / 15g. (recommended) .... fire
Radicchio 1 head / 30g. (recommended) .... fire
Tomato 15 pieces (diced) / 100g. (recommended)..................... wood
Olive oil 1 table spoon / 10g. (recommended)............................ earth
Olives 2 table spoons / 16g. (yes)... fire
Vinegar Aceto Balsamico 1 table spoon / 10g. (recommended) . wood
Mustard medium hot 2 teaspoons / 5g. (recommended) ....metal
Sesame paste (Tahini) 1 teaspoon / 2g. (yes)........................... earth
Parmesan 2 table spoons / 20g. (little).................................... earth
Salt 1 pinch / 0,5g. (recommended)...water
Pepper (ground) 1 pinch / 0,2g. (little)......................................metal
Rosemary 2 teaspoons / 3g. () .... fire

Cooking instructions:
Wash the salad, pluck it small and arrange it in a bowl.

Sauce: Put the oil, the balsamic vinegar, the mustard and the tahini in a
glass with a lid and shake well. Season the dressing with salt and
pepper. Mix the salad with the salad dressing and the olives, sprinkle
with parmesan and finally with rosemary.

7.33 Tae from Dandelionroots

Cools liver fire, reduces internal heat, softens knots.
Cooking time approx. 15 min
Calories p. portion: 1
2 portions

Quantity of ingredients
Dandelion (young plants) 2-4 teaspoons / 6g. (recommended) ..... fire
Water 2 cup / 500g. (yes).. earth

Cooking instructions:
The chopped dandelion is doused with cold water. Heat the whole thing until it boils and cook for a minute. Then let it rest for ten minutes, filter and enjoy ... Sweet to taste with honey.

7.34 Tea from celery sticks

Brings the Liver Qi in motion, cools heat, moisturizes, relaxes, builds up Qi, spreads.
Cooking time approx. 15 min
Calories p. portion: 1
4 portions
Allergens: L

Quantity of ingredients
Celery sticks 2 table spoons (chopped) / 18g. (recommended) .. earth
Water 2 cup / 500g. (yes).. earth

Cooking instructions:
Heat the water till it boils and put it aside. Add cutted celery and cook for 10 min. to let go. Strain. Sweet to taste with honey.

7.35 Tea from elderberry blossom tea

Derives wind-cold and wind-heat.
Cooking time approx. 10 min
Calories p. portion: 7
4 portions

Quantity of ingredients
Elderberry blossom tee 4 teaspoons / 12g. (recommended) .... fire
Water 2 cup / 500g. (yes).. earth

Cooking instructions:
Heat the water till it boils and put it aside. Add elderberry blossom tea and 10 min. to let go. Sweet to taste with honey. Strain when pouring.

7.36 Tea from lavender blossoms

Cooking time approx. 10 min
Calories p. portion: 0
1 portions

Quantity of ingredients
Lavender blossoms 1 teaspoon / 2g. (recommended).....................*
Water 1 cup / 125g. (yes)....................................... earth

Cooking instructions:
Heat the water till it boils and put it aside. Add lavender flowers and 10 min. to let go. Sweet to taste with honey. Strain when pouring.

7.37 Tea from mallow

Preserves the fluids, contracts, cools liver fire, forces stomach-Yin. Dissolves mucus of the pores of the heart.
Cooking time approx. 10 min
Calories p. portion: 0
4 portions

Quantity of ingredients
Mallow (Malva sylvestris) blossom tea 2 teabags / 4g. (little) ....*
Water 2 cup / 500g. (yes)....................................... earth

Cooking instructions:
Heat the water till it boils and put it aside. Add mallow tee and 10 min. to let go. Sweet to taste with honey. Strain when pouring.

7.38 Tea from Melissa

Preserves the fluids, contracts, soothes liver fire, stimulates lungs Qi.
Cooking time approx. 10 min
Calories p. portion: 0
4 portions

Quantity of ingredients
Balm 2 teaspoons / 4g. (recommended) ....wood
Water 2 cup / 500g. (yes)....................................... earth

Cooking instructions:
Heat the water till it boils and put it aside. Add lemon balm and 10 min. to let go. Sweet to taste with honey. Strain when pouring.

7.39 Tea from sage

Distributes mucus, passes downwardly, activates Wei Qi, forces Qi.
Cooking time approx. 15 min
Calories p. portion: 4
4 portions

Quantity of ingredients
Sage 2 teaspoons / 6g. (recommended).. fire
Water 2 cup / 500g. (yes)... earth

Cooking instructions:
Heat the water till it boils and put it aside. Add sage and 10 min. to let go. Strain. Sweet to taste with honey.

7.40 Tea Green tea

Reduces internal heat, dissolves mucus, detoxifies.
Cooking time approx. 10 min
Calories p. portion: 2
1 portions

Quantity of ingredients
Green tea 1 teaspoon / 2g. (recommended) .... fire
Water 1 cup / 120g. (yes).. earth

Cooking instructions:
For each cup you use a teaspoonful or a teabag.
Pour green tea only with 60 to 80 ° C / 140 to 176 °F hot water, otherwise it will be bitter.
If the tea has a stimulating effect, let it draw for two to three minutes. It has a calming effect for a duration of five minutes (no longer, otherwise it will be bitter!).
Another method: Pour the tea leaves with about 70 ° C / 158 °F hot water and pour the water immediately again. Then just pour hot water again. The bitter substances disappear and the tea gets a milder aroma.

7.41 Tea mixture against bile ailments

Preserves the fluids, contracts, soothes liver fire, stimulates lungs Qi.
Cooking time approx. 10 min
Calories p. portion: 0
4 portions

Quantity of ingredients
Balm 1 teaspoon / 0,4g. (recommended) .... wood
Dyer's broom herb 1/2 oz / 0,4g. (recommended) .... *
Wormwood 1/8 oz / 0,4g. (recommended) .... fire
Agrimony 1/8 oz / 0,4g. (recommended) .... metal
Hop 1/8 oz / 0,4g. (recommended) .... *
Water 2 cups / 500g. (yes) .... earth

Cooking instructions:
Add 1 tablespoon of the mixture to 1 cup of boiling water, infuse for 10 minutes, strain, drink ½ cup 4 times a day!

7.42 Wheat fresh grain porridge with pears.

Moisturizes lungs, cools heat, reduces lung mucus, nourishes Yin from heart and kidney, forces heart and kidney, moisturizes, relaxes, builds up Qi, spreads.
Cooking time approx. 25 min
Calories p. portion: 309
2 portions
Allergens: ANO

Quantity of ingredients
Wheat 1 cup / 100g. (recommended) .... wood
Water 2-4 cups / 350g. (yes) .... earth
Pear 2 pieces / 300g. (recommended) .... earth
Raisins 1 table spoon / 10g. () .... earth
Sesame, white 1 table spoon / 8g. (recommended) .... earth
Sunflower seeds 1 table spoon / 8g. (yes) .... earth
Cardamom 1 pinch / 0,3g. (recommended) .... *
Salt 1 pinch / 0,3g. (recommended) .... water

Cooking instructions:
Preparation the night before: Wheat roughly cut; soak overnight.
In the morning: Put the wheat meal with a little hot water; simmer with stirring for about 15 minutes.
Meanwhile, add pear compote, raisins, crushed sesame, sunflower

seeds, some ground cardamom, a small pinch of salt.
Variants: with grated apple or seasonal fruit.

8 Effects of food

8.1 Use ingredients: recommendable

Acai powder
Acerola fruit nectar or powder
Agar agar (kelp)
Agave nectar
Agrimony
Almond
Aloe juice
Amaranth Pops
Angelica root
Apple (sweet)
Apple juice (natural cloudy)
Apple puree
Apricot dried
Apricot jam
Apricot nectar
Apricots juice
Arrowroot
Artichoke
Baking powder
Balm
Banchatee (green tea)
barberry
Barley flour
Barley grass powder
Barley grouts
Barley malt
Barley not peeled
Basic recipe for a beef soup
Basic recipe for a beef soup (warming)
Basic recipe for a chicken soup
(warming)
Basic recipe for a duck soup
Basic recipe for a fish soup
Basic recipe for a rice soup (Congee)
Basic recipe for a vegetable soup
(nutritious)
Bay leaf
Beans (green, fresh)
Bearberry leaf
Beef bone marrow
Beef heart
Beef heart (calf)
Beef kidney
Beef liver

Beef lungs (calf)
Beef Oxtail pieces
Beef soup meat
Beer (alcohol-free)
Beer (alcohol-reduced)
Beer (Pils)
Beer (Top-fermented German dark beer)
Berries of the season
Berry juice
Bitter Herb liqueur
Bitter Lemon
Bitter liqueur
Bitter orange peel
Black beans
Black caraway
Black fungus mushroom
Blackberry dried (unripe fruit)
Blackberry jam
Blackberry leaves
Blackthorn (Sloe)
Blue mallow tee
Blueberry dried
Blueberry jam
Bocksdorn fruits (Fructus Lycii, Goji, goji berry dried
Boletus mushroom
Borage
Borage oil
Brazil nuts
Bread roll
Bread with carob kernel flour
Breadcrumbs (wheat bread, bread roll)
Brie cheese
Broad beans (thick beans)
Broccoli
Brown ale
Brussels sprouts
Buckbean
Buckwheat
Buckwheat (roasted) Kasha
Buckwheat whole grain
Bush beans
Butter (half fat)

Butter beans white
Butter organic
Calamari
Camembert
Campari
Capers in olive oil
Cardamom
Carob flour, St. john's bread
Carp
Carrot (Early Carrot)
Cashews
Cauliflower
Celery root
Celery sticks
Chamomile
Chamomile tea
Champignon
Channa-Dal
Chanterelle
Chenpi (chinese tangerine bowl)
Cherry (sour)
Cherry compote
Chervil
Chervil dried
Chestnut puree
Chicken Blood
Chicken egg
Chicken egg white
Chicken heart
Chicken stomach
Chicken yolk
Chickpeas
Chickweed
Chicory
Chinese cabbage
Chinese pearl barley
Chlorella (fresh water)
Chocolate
Chocolate (Diabetic)
Chrysanthemum blossom tea
Clarified butter
Clementine
Coconut fat
Coconut flakes
Coconut grated
Coconut meat
Codfish
Coix (seeds) YiYi Ren
Cola drink
Cola drink (low calorie)
Compote (fruits of the season)
Cooking oil
Coriander (fresh)
Corn

Corn (fast polenta)
Corn (roasted)
Corn flour
Corn germ oil
Corn silk tea
Corn starch
Cottage cheese
Cranberries
Cranberry
Cranberry jam
Cream (30% fat)
Cream 10% coffee cream
Cream sour 10%
Cream sour 20%
Cream sour 30%
Creamer
Créme fraiche cheese
Crispbread
Crucian
Cucumber
Cucumber (bitter)
Cucumber (spicy cucumber)
Currant jam (black)
Currant jam (red)
Currant juice (black)
Currants (black)
Currants (red)
Curry paste red
Daisy
Dandelion (young plants)
Dandelion juice
Dashi
Dates red
Deer's Bones
Deer's kidneys
Duck (heart)
Duck (slaughtered)
Ducks egg
Dulse (seaweed)
Dyer's broom herb
Edam cheese
Eel smoked
Elderberries
Elderberry blossom tee
Emmental cheese
Endive salad
Evening primrose oil
Fennel seeds ground
Fenugreek (Trigonella foenum-
graecum)
Fernet Branca (herbal bitter liqueur)
Feta cheese
Fig
Fig dried

Fish innards
Fish pieces mixed (fresh water)
Fish remains
Fish sauce
Flounder
Flower pollen
Fox nut, gorgon nut, makhana
Fresh cheese from soya
Fresh cheese with herbs
Freshwater crab
Freshwater fish
Fructose (glucose)
Fruit mix juice
Fruit tea
Gail plum
Galangal
Garam Masala powder
Gelatin white
Gelee Royal
Gentian root
Gentian root tea
Ginger oil
Ginkgo fruit
Ginseng
Ginseng liqueur
Ginseng root
Goat and sheep's blood
Goat and sheep's brain
Goat and sheep's liver
Goat and sheep's stomach
Goose
Goose blood
Goose fat
Goose parts
Gorgonzola
Gouda cheese
Gourd
Grape juice red
Grape juice white
Grapefruit dried peel
Grapes red
Grapeseed oil
Green tea
Greengage
Ground
Ground caraway
Guava
Halibut (Flatfish)
Hazelnuts
Herbal tea mix
Herbs bitter
Herbs of Provence
Herbs various
Herbs wild

Herring
Hibiscus
Hibiscus tea
Hijiki
Hokkaido pumpkin
Honey wine (Met)
Hop
Horehound leaves
Horse meat
Iceberg lettuce
Jasmine blossoms tee
Jellyfish
Kaki plum
Kalmus
Kidney beans (red)
King Solomon's-seal
Kombu seaweed (Saccharina japonica)
Kudzu
Kukicha tea
Ladyfingers
Lamb kidneys
Lamb liver
Lamb's lettuce
Lavender blossoms
Leaf salads (bitter)
Lemon Balm (dried)
Lemon Balm (fresh)
Lemongrass
Lentils black
Lentils red
Licorice root tea
Lily bulbs
Lima beans
Lime blossom tea
Linseed
Linseed (crushed)
Linseed oil
Liver smoothing tea
Loquate / Japanese medlar
Lotus roots
Lotus seeds
Lovage seeds
Luo Han Guo fruit
Lychee liqueur
Lye roll
Mackerel
Malt
Mango juice
Manioc flour
Maple syrup
Mare's milk
Margarine
Margarine (diet)
Martini

Mascarpone cheese
Mayonnaise 50%
Mayonnaise 80%
Mediterranean fish (cod, plaice, haddock, sea eel, mackerel)
Medlar
Millet
Millet flakes
Mineral water
Mirabelle plum
Miso
Miso black (fermented)
Mixed Pickles
Morel (black, dried)
Morel, dried
Mu Erh Mushroom
Muesli
Mulled Wine Spice
Multi-grain bread (gray bread)
Mung bean
Mustard
Mustard Dijon
Mustard medium hot
Mustard seeds
Mustard sweet
Nasturtium (nose-twister or nose-tweaker)
Nectarine
Nettles
Noodles (wheat) with egg
Noodles (wheat, lasagne) with egg
Noodles (wheat, ribbon noodles) with egg
Noodles (wheat, spaghetti) with egg
Noodles (whole grain) with egg
Nori, purple seaweed, red algae
Oat flakes roasted
Oat milk
Octopus
Octopus
Olive oil
Olives green
Orange blossom
Orange dried peel
Orange grated peel
Orange jam
Orange peel
Oregano fresh
Oyster shell powder
Oysters
Palm oil
Parsley root
Parsnip
Passion blossoms tea

Passion fruit
Peanut (roasted)
Peanut butter
Peanut oil
Peanuts
Pear
Pearl barley
Pearl barley
Peas, green
Pepper powder (hot)
Peppermint
Peppermint tea
Pepperoni
Pepperoni, red, pitted, halved
Pepperoni, yellow, pitted, halved
Peppers (sweet)
Peppers powder
Perch
Pickle
Pig blood
Pigeon egg
Pine nuts
Pinto beans speckled
Pistachios
Plum dried
Plums
Pork Bacon
Pork brain
Pork fat (lard)
Pork ham
Pork ham cooked
Pork ham smoked
Pork kidneys
Pork Lard
Pork lung
Pork marrow bones
Pork sausage (Bratwurst) Pork/beef sausage (smoked)
Pork's intestine
Potato
Potato (mealy)
Potato flour
Prickly pear
Processed cheese 12%
processed cheese 30%
Prosecco
Psyllium seed
Pudding powder vanilla
Puff pastry
Pumpernickel (dark bread)
Pumpkin seeds
Quail
Quail egg
Quince

Quinoa
Rabbit (wild)
Radicchio
Radish horseradish
Radish leaves
Rapeseed oil
Raspberry jam
Raspberry leaf tea
Red beet
Red berry (without sugar)
Red cabbage
Reishi mushroom
Ribworttea
Rice (Gaoliang / Sorghum)
Rice Basmati
Rice long grain rice
Rice mash
Rice starch
Rice sticky
Romaine lettuce / lettuce salad
Rose blossom tea
Rose hip
Rose leaf tea
Rosefish
Rucola
Rum
Rusk
Rye
Rye flour
Rye wholemeal bread
Safflower (Dyer's thistle / Hong Hua)
Saffron
Sage
Salmon
Salt
Salt (herbal)
Savory
Savoy cabbage / kale
Sea buckthorn
Sea cucumber
Sesame oil
Sesame oil roasted
Sesame, black
Sesame, white
Shark
Sheep's milk
Sheep's milk yoghurt
Sherry (whine)
Shiitake, dried
Shrimps
Skim milk powder
Slug
Sourdough
Soy flour

Soy noodles
Soy Tofu
Soy Tofu smoked
Soya Cuisine (soy cream)
Soybean milk
Soybeans
Soybeans, black
Soybeans, blacks, fermented
Soybeans, yellow
Spelled flakes
Spirit
Spurdog (spiny dogfish, Schillerlocken)
St. Benedict's thistle, blessed thistle,
holy thistle, spotted thistle
Stevia (candyleaf, sweetleaf)
Strawberry jam
Sugar - icing sugar
Sugar palm sugar
Sugar substitute (sweetener)
Sunflower oil
Supplementary nutrition
Tabasco
Tarragon (Estragon)
Tea mixture uric acid lowering
Thistle oil
Thyme dried
Toast bread (whole grain)
Tomato
Tomato dried
Tomato juice
Tomato paste
Tomato puree
Tonic Water
Trout
Trout (smoked)
Truffle
Tsampa (roasted barley flour)
Turkey ham
Turmeric (yellow root)
Turnip
Turnips
Umeboshi paste
Valerian
Vanilla
Vanilla pod
Vanilla powder
Vanilla sugar natural
Vegetable juice
Vinegar (Red wine vinegar)
Vinegar Aceto Balsamico
Vinegar Aceto Balsamico white
Wakame
Walnut oil
Walnuts roasted

Watermelon
Wax gourd
Wheat
Wheat bulgur
Wheat flakes
Wheat flatbread/pita bread
Wheat flour
Wheat flour whole grain
Wheat germ oil
Wheat semolina
Wheat semolina for children
Wheat/Rye/Gray-black bread with yeast
Wheatgrass juice
Wheatgrass powder
Whey
White beans
White bread (baguette)
White bread (pretzel sticks)
White bread (roll)

White bread (wheat bread)
White breadcrumbs
White cabbage
White dumpling bread (wheat bread cut into chunks)
Whitefish
Whole grain bread
Wholemeal flour
Wild garlic (garlic spinach)
Wild herbs
Wild strawberries
Wormwood
Wormwood herb
Yam root, yam root tuber
Yarrow
Yeast
Yew nut
Yoghurt vanilla
Zucchini

8.2   Use ingredients: yes

Amaranth
Asparagus (green or white)
Aubergine
Avocado
Bamboo shoots
Banana
Banana (cooking banana)
Barley
Batavia
Black tea
Black-eyed peas
Burdock root tea
Cantaloupe
Carambola (Star fruit)
Caviar
Chard
Crab
Cress
Dandelionroots tea
Grapefruit (Pomelo)
Grapefruit juice
Honey
Kiwi
Lamb's lettuce
Lemon
Lemon juice
Lemon peel
Lettuce
Lime
Mango
Miso paste (soy bean paste)
Mulberry fruit

Mullet
Mung bean sprouting
Mussels
Olives
Orange
Orange juice
Peas
Plum
Rabbit
Rabbit liver
Radish black
Rhubarb
Rice (fragrance)
Rice (whole grain)
Rice black
Rice flour
Rice noodles
Rice red
Rice round grain
Rice sweet
Rice variety any
Rice wild (nature rice)
Salsify
Seacrab
Sesame paste (Tahini)
Sorrel
Soy sauce
Spinach
Sugar molasses
Sunflower seeds
Sweet potato
Topinambur

Water
Water hot
Wheat beer
Wheat bran

Yarrow tea
Yogurt (natural, 1.5% fat)
Yogurt (natural, 3.5% fat)

8.3   Use ingredients: little

Adzuki beans
Anise (Common Fennel)
Apple (sour)
Blackberry´s
Blueberry
Blueberry juice
Bulgur (cereals)
Buttermilk
Chives
Clementines
Clove
Coriander
Couscous
Cow's milk (1.5% fat)
Cow's milk (whole milk 3.5% fat)
Cranberry
Cranberry juice
Cream, sweet 30%
Cumin (Caraway seed)
Curd cheese 20%
Curd cheese 40%
Currant (black)
Currant (red)
Currant (white)
Deer meat
Dill
Fennel tea
Fresh cheese
Ginger fresh
Gooseberry
Grapes white
Hawthorn
Kefir
Leek
Lentils
Lentils yellow
Lychee
Lychee in Preserved
Mallow (Malva sylvestris) blossom tea
Marjoram
Mozzarella
Onion (spring onion)
Onion read
Onion white
Parmesan

Pear juice
Pepper (ground)
Pepper Cayenne
Pepper white (ground)
Peppercorns
Pheasant
Pigeon
Pineapple
Pineapple (from a can)
Pineapple juice without sugar
Pork heart
Pork knuckle
Pork liver
Pork meat
Pork skin
Pork stomach
Rabbit meat
Raspberry
Raspberry dried (immature)
Sauerkraut (cutted cabbage fermented)
Sour cherries
Sour cream 15% fat
Sour milk
Sour milk cheese 20%
Spelled (Dark) bread
Spelled grain
Spelled semolina
Spelled wholemeal flour
Star anise
Strawberries
Strawberry Juice
Sugar brown
Sugar candy white
Sugar cane sugar
Sugar fructose - fruit sugar
Sugar glucose - grapes sugar
Sugar Milk Sugar
Sugar white
Tangerine
Wild boar meat

8.4 Do not use contra-acting foods

Almond marzipan
Almond milk
Almond puree
Anchovy / Sardine
Apricot
Apricots
Basil
Basil (fresh)
Bean oil
Beef fillet
Beef meat
Beef meat (calf)
Beef meatbones
Beef stomach
Boxhorn clover seeds
Carrot
Carrot juice without sugar
Cereal coffee
Cherry
Cherry juice
Chestnuts
Chicken liver
Chicken meat
Chili (pod or ground)
Cinnamon ground
Cinnamon sticks
Cocoa
Coconut milk
Cod
Coffee
Corn Grease (Polenta)
Curcuma
Curry
Dates dried
Deer meat
Eel
Fennel
Feta cheese
French beans
Garlic
Ginger powder
Goat
Goat and sheep's milk
Goat cheese
Goose egg
Grass carp
Green spelt
Hyssop
Juniper berry
Kohlrabi
Kumquats

Lamb bones
Lamb meat
Lamb shoulder
Lobster
Longane
Lovage
Mold cheese
Mutton
Mutton
Nutmeg
Oat
Oat flakes (whole grain)
Oat flour
Oat fusion (baby food)
Oat meal
Okra
Onion (shallot)
Oregano dried
Oyster mushroom
Papaya
Parsley
Peaches
Peaches (canned)
Peppers
Peppers (rose peppers)
Pimento
Plaice
Pomegranate
Poppy
Pumpkin
Pumpkin seed oil
Radish
Radish (white, green, purple-red)
Raisins
Red wine
Rice malt
Rose hip tea
Rosemary
Sago (cereals)
Sake
Shrimp
Soybean oil
Spiny lobsters
Thyme
Tuna
Turkey breast meat
Umeboshi plums (Japanese apricots)
Vinegar (Apple vinegar)
Walnuts
White wine
Yogi tea

9 Herbs and their effects

9.1 Basil

thermal effect: warm
taste: spicy, bitter
Dries out, leads down. Tonifies Yang and Qi, dissolves mucus-cold, eliminates wind-cold.
It has a beneficial effect on flatulence and nausea, relaxing and soothing. Good to fight emphysema, bronchitis, whooping cough, high blood pressure, headache, mouth odor, warts, hiccup, gout, migraine.

9.2 Birch leaves

thermal effect: cool
taste: bitter
Induces moisture, diuretic, eliminates wind-cold / heat-moisture, eliminates heat.
This tea is diuretic and helps to fight kidney ailments, gout and cleans the blood, also helps with bacterial and inflammatory urinary tract diseases, kidney grief and rheumatic complaints.

9.3 Dill

thermal effect: warm
taste: spicy
Moves qi, triggers stagnation, heads up.
The medicinal and spice herb has an antispasmodic effect and stimulates gastric juice production. Good to fight flatulence. Antispasmodic for gastrointestinal discomfort.

9.4 Dyer's broom herb

thermal effect: neutral
taste: bitter
Emanates moisture, diuretic, regulates and moves qi, regulates bowel movement / laxative, eliminates wind-cold / heat-wetness.
The Herb is used as a diuretic (for the purge of water) and for digestion. Due to the side effects, birch leaves or dandelions are recommended rather than the Dyer broom, which have very similar effects, but are not toxic.

9.5 Hop

thermal effect: cold
taste: bitter
Eliminates heat caused by yin deficiency, soothes mind / spirit, eliminates heat and dries wet, regulates qi. Suppresses inner wind, tonifies Qi.
Calming, hormone-regulating, appetizing, strengthens the stomach and intestines, diuretic, pain-relieving and antispasmodic.

9.6 Coriander

thermal effect: warm
taste: spicy
Driving sweat, reducing wind, draining moisture, tonifying and regulating qi, eliminating wind-cold.
The essential oils are appetizing, digestive, cramping and soothing in stomach and intestinal disorders.

9.7 Herbs various

Stimulates appetite. Effect different.
Appetizing, lots of trace elements and vitamins.

9.8 Cress

thermal effect: cool
taste: sweet
Moves and tonifies qi and blood, diuretic, cools in internal heat, moisturizes lungs, triggers stagnation, heads upwards.
Diuretic, supports urination. Good to fight dry mouth, inner agitation, sore throat, diabetes, kidney stones, gastrointestinal complaints, lung problems, menstrual cramps or cancer.

9.9 Chives

thermal effect: warm
taste: spicy
Directs upward. Tonifies blood, kidney Yang and Qi. Dissolves moisture.
Bactericide, prevents cancer, strengthens gastric juice production, promotes digestion and blood circulation, promotes growth, triggers stagnation.

9.10 Lavender blossoms

thermal effect: warm
taste: spicy, bitter
Do not use during pregnancy. Suppresses internal wind, dissipates
moisture and heat. Regulates and moves Qi, tones Qi, moves blood,
eliminates heat, reduces fire.
Calms the central nervous system, relieves anxiety, to fight sleep
disturbances, loss of appetite and nervous intestinal complaints.

9.11 Lily bulbs

thermal effect: cool
taste: sweet, bitter
Tonifies Yin, soothes Shen / Spirit. Moisturizes the lungs, clears heat and
stops coughing.
Calms nerves, good to fight scaly skin. The onions and the petals are
added to ointments in the Orient, which can heal muscles and tendons.
White lily (astringent).

9.12 Dandelion (young plants)

thermal effect: cool
taste: sweet, bitter
Cools liver-heat, reduces internal heat, softens knots, eliminates heat,
reduces fire, dissolves mucus heat, moves blood, tonifies qi.
Detoxifies, relieves inflammation. Regulates digestion, helps with
rheumatism, releases kidney stones, leaves pimples and chronic skin
disorders disappear.

9.13 Balm

thermal effect: warm
taste: bitter
Keep the fluids, pulls together, soothe lever fire, soothe Shen, stimulate
Lung Qi. Regulates qi, eliminates heat caused by yin deficiency.
Soothing effect, Good for insomnia, restlessness and upset stomach,
Allergies, Asthma, Migraine, Flatulence, Headache, Rheumatism and
mental tension. To strengthen after cold and infectious diseases.

9.14 Agrimony

thermal effect: neutral
taste: bitter
Astringent, regulates and moves qi, eliminates heat, reduces fire, dissipates moisture / moisture, tones qi.
Good to fight persistent rheumatism, bedwetting, some mouth sores and spleen disease. For the treatment of wounds and inflammations of the skin as envelopes.

9.15 Rosemary

thermal effect: warm
taste: bitter
Dries out, leads down. Strengthens the heart, lungs and spleen qi, strengthens liver blood. Strengthens heart-Yin. Expels spleen heat / cold moisture. Strengthens spleen and kidney yang.
Promotes digestion, relieves bloating, strengthens lung, spleen and kidney. Affects the circulation and nerves. Appetizing. Baths help to fight circulatory disorders as well as with gout and rheumatism.

9.16 Sage

thermal effect: neutral
taste: bitter, spicy
Expels slime, guides down, strengthens Qi, eliminates Wind-Heat, eliminate heat induced by Yin deficiency.
Good to fight yeast infections. The leaves have a digestive effect and are used in greasy foods. Antiperspirant effect. Helps to relieve coughing attacks. Dries out.

9.17 King Solomon's-seal

thermal effect: neutral
taste: sweet, bitter
Tonifies Yin and Qi, astringent, tonifies blood, eliminates wind-cold / heat-wetness.
Used to repair wounds or damaged tissue. Good to fight dry cough, earlier also tuberculosis and dysentery, as well as diarrhea and hemorrhoids.

9.18 Yam root, yam root tuber

thermal effect: neutral
taste: sweet
Tonifies Yin, Yang and Qi, reduces inner wind, dissolves wetness, warms Yang.
Solves cramps (in the gastrointestinal tract). Digestive through increased bile production. Anti-inflammatory in rheumatic diseases.
Mucolytic agent for coughing. Relief of menopausal symptoms.

10 Basics of Nutrition

The basic principles of nutrition described herein are general recommendations. They are not aimed at a specific form of therapy. Recommendations concerning a therapy have priority.

10.1 Nutrition

Regular meals in a relaxed atmosphere. A warm breakfast is considered a good start into the day.
The main meals ought to be taken for lunch – supper in the early evening. Pay attention to feeling hungry or sated: don't eat too much nor remain hungry is the rule
Prepare the meals freshly from natural, regional products. Frozen, heat-conserved, industrially prepared or foodstuffs cooked in the microwave oven are rejected.
Choice of foodstuffs according to the season: more cooling food in summer, more warming food in winter.
Eat cooked food at least twice a day. Food and drinks ought to be lukewarm, never ice-cold or hot.
Raw vegetables, briefly cooked vegetables, freshly squeezed juices and mineral water are not recommended. Milk and dairy products are only included in the diet if they don't cause problems. Don't use therapeutic recipes over a longer period without consulting your doctor or therapist.

Varied food
Enjoy the diversity of foodstuffs. Characteristics of a balanced nutrition are variety, suitable combination and a balanced quantity of rich and low energy foodstuffs (on one hand avoiding undersupply with essential nutrients and on the other hand to take to many undesirable substances).

A lot of Cereal Products - and Potatoes
Bread, pasta, rice, cereal flakes (best wholemeal) as well as potatoes contain almost no fat, but many vitamins, mineral nutrients, trace elements, roughage and secondary plant substances. These foodstuffs ought to be taken with low-fat side dishes.

Vegetables and Fruit – „Take Five" every day ... 5 portions of vegetables and fruit a day, as fresh as possible, briefly cooked, or maybe one portion as a juice – ideal as a side dish to every meal as well as snack between meals: Thus a lot of vitamins, mineral nutrients as well as roughage and secondary plant substances

Daily milk and dairy products
Milk and Dairy Products every Day, once or twice per Week Fish; meat, sausages as well as eggs moderately. These foodstuffs contain valuable nutrients like calcium in the milk, iodine selenium and omega-3 fat acids in saltwater fish. Meat is favorable due to its high content of disposable iron and the vitamins B1, B6 and B12. Quantities of 300 – 600 g meat and sausage per week are sufficient. Prefer low-fat products, especially in meat- and dairy products.

Low-fat and fatty Foodstuffs
Fat supplies us with essential fat acids and fatty foodstuffs contain also fat-soluble vitamins. Fat is high in energy; therefore much fat in the food may cause overweight, possibly also cancer. Too many saturated fat acids may further a tendency for cardio-vascular diseases in the long term. Prefer vegetable oils and fats (e.g. rapeseed-, olive-, soya-oils and solid fats produced therefrom). Beware of invisible fat in meat- and dairy products, pastry and sweets as well as in fast-food and convenience foods. 70 – 90 g fat per day is sufficient.

Moderately Sugar and Salt
Take sugar and foods/drinks containing various kinds of sugar (e.g. glucose syrup) only occasionally. Use herbs and spices as well as a little salt creatively. Prefer salt containing iodine.

Plenty of Liquids
Water is absolutely essential. Drink 1-2 l liquids every day. Prefer water (with or without gas) and other low-calorie drinks. Alcoholic drinks should not be taken.

Tasty Dishes, carefully cooked
Cook the meals with as low temperatures and as short as possible, using little water and fat – this preserves the original taste, keeps the nutrients intact and prevents the production of harmful compounds.

Take time and enjoy the food
Take your Time and enjoy your Food
Eating consciously helps to eat right. The eye enjoys food, too. It's fun, invites to enjoy varied dishes and stimulates the feeling of satiety.

Watch your Weight and stay in Motion
A balanced diet and a lot of exercise and sport (30 – 60 min/day) are a healthy combination. The right weight furthers well-being and health. Thermals, directional effectiveness, digestive power

There are various criteria for judging the effectiveness of herbs and foodstuffs.

The use of certain herbs and ingredients is based on observations of the effects on the body which these foodstuffs, herbs and spices show after having eaten them. The medical science has developed following system: Every ingredient or herb has a directional effectiveness. Furthermore, there are herbs which have a special effect on certain organs.

The basic condition for a healthy metabolism is to obtain sufficient energy from food and that the digestive process doesn't use too much energy. An easily digestible meal makes content and sated, doesn't cause flatulence and fatigue after the meal. The perfect spices increase the healthiness of our meals. Very often, just small doses of herbs and spices will suffice. They are not used to make us sated, but to help our digestive organs to digest the food.

10.2 Recipes

The recipes list the ingredients to be used and the cooking instructions show how the dish is prepared. The list of ingredients shows the concerned quantities as well as the relevance for the therapy. If you find „less than mentioned", try to comply or find an alternative from the „list of recommended foodstuffs". Mostly it shall result just in a small change of taste when you simply avoid this ingredient.

Mild cooking methods: boiling, stewing, poaching, steaming
Strong cooking methods: barbecuing, roasting, frying, smoking
Balanced cooking methods: deep-frying, baking brick
Deep-freezing and warming in the microwave oven should be avoided (denaturalization).

10.3 Foodstuffs

Foodstuffs have an effect on body and soul like medicinal herbs, only a very much milder one. Dietary advice is mainly based on regional foodstuffs. The knowledge about the effects of each foodstuff and the knowledge, when which foodstuff shall be used, is based on the orthodox school of medicine. Use ecologic-organic products, if possible. As everything should be cooked for a long time due to a better digestability and very rarely eaten raw, the food agrees with everyone.

The classification of the foodstuffs according to their effect on the body is the basis in order to achieve a harmonious status of health.

Dietary advisors do not recommend certain foodstuffs for everyone. The individual diet is tailor-made for the individual constitution.

Buy only fresh and ripe fruit and vegetables. You ought to leave unripe fruit and vegetables and such with brown spots and wilted leaves behind in the market. In this case take deep-frozen goods (never ready-to-serve dishes!). Fruit and vegetables are deep-frozen immediately after harvesting and often contain more vitamins and minerals than the goods from the vegetable shelf. Whereas conserved or tinned goods contain very much less biological substances. Also, salt, sugar and others are mostly added to the latter. Never leave the foodstuffs in the water after washing them to avoid that many vital substances get drowned. Clean salads, fruit and vegetables immediately before serving.

Please make sure of the hygienic processing of foodstuffs. Clean your salads, fruit and vegetables carefully. When cooking with meat, prepare all ingredients first and then process the meat products. Clean the worktop and tools very carefully. Wooden surfaces ought to be treated with a mild disinfectant regularly in order to reduce germination.
Store fruit and vegetables separately, if possible. Harvested fruit and vegetables are still alive and emit e.g. ethylene gas, which makes other products ripen and age faster. Keep meat and fish in the closed packaging or store them in the fridge in closed containers.

10.4 Herbs

There are some basic rules for storing medicinal herbs. On principle, herbs must be protected from direct sunlight, humidity and heat.

Containers for the storage of herbs may be glasses, ceramic jars and even plastic containers. However, plastic is a rather unsuitable material and should only be a short-term solution. In case of glass containers, use a dark material.

Medicinal herbs cannot be kept for any long period. The shelf life of herbs is limited. However, it can be prolonged with suitable storage. The place should be dark, rather cool and absolutely dry. A wooden medicine cabinet, placed not directly next to a source of heat, would be ideal. Never buy large quantities of herbs so as not to have to throw them away. Label the container with the name of the herb and the date of harvesting or processing.

11 Other dietic-books

The following syndromes of dietetics, TCM or for a therapy supplement for cancer are available.

Dietetics
E001. Nutrition of the infant - baby food
E002. Nutrition during lactation
E003. Nutrition in old age
E004. Nutrition of children and adolescents
E005. Nutrition of athletes
E006. Light weight
E007. Pregnancy
E008. Full food

Protein and electrolyte - kidneys
E009. (hemodialysis) dialysis treatment
E010. Acute renal failure
E011. Chronic renal insufficiency
E012. Nephrotic syndrome
E013. Kidney stones (nephrolithiasis)

Gastrointestinal tract - pancreas
E014. Acute pancreatitis (inflammation of the pancreas)
E015. Chronic pancreatitis (inflammation of the pancreas)

Gastrointestinal tract - small intestine and large intestine
E016. Acute obstipation (constipation)
E017. Chronic obstipation (constipation)
E018. Colon irritabile
E019. Diverticulitis
E020. Acquired lactose intolerance (lactose malabsorption)
E021. Fructose malabsorption
E022. Glutensensitive enteropathy (celiac disease)
E023. Colectomy
E024. Short Bowel Syndrome

Gastrointestinal tract - liver, gallbladder, bile ducts
E025. Acute and chronic hepatitis (inflammation of the liver)
E026. Cholelithiasis (bile stones)
E027. fatty liver
E028. cirrhosis

Gastrointestinal tract - Stomach and duodenal intestine
E029. Acute gastritis
E030. Chronic gastritis
E031. Stomach bleeding
E032. Ulcus ventriculi and duodenal ulcer
E033. Condition after gastric surgery

Gastrointestinal tract - oral cavity and esophagus
E034. Stomatitis
E035. Esophageal carcinoma (esophageal cancer)
E036. Refluosophagitis (heartburn)

Special diseases
E037. Phenylketonuria (PKU)
E038. Rheumatic joint diseases

Metabolism
E039. Obesity (overweight)
E040. Diabetes mellitus
E041. Eating disorders (underweight)

Fat metabolism
E042. Hypercholesterolaemia (increased cholesterol level)
E043. Hepatic Encephalopathy

Heart and circulation
E044. Arteriosclerosis (arterial calcification)
E045. Heart insufficiency
E046. Hypertension
E047. Hyperuricaemia and gout

Changed nutrient requirements
E048. In case of fever
E049. For malignant diseases
E050. After burns
E051. Radiation and chemotherapy

CANCER
E100. Pancreatic cancer
E101. Bladder cancer
E102. Blood cancer (leukemia)
E103. Breast cancer
E104. Colorectal cancer
E105. Gastric cancer
E106. Kidney cancer
E107. Esophageal cancer

TCM
E200. Bladder - moisture heat in the bladder
E201. Bladder - moisture and cold in the bladder
E202. Bladder - emptiness and cold in the bladder
E203. Large intestine - external cold affects the large intestine
E204. Large intestine - moisture heat in the large intestine
E205. Large intestine - heat blocks the intestine II acute
E206. Large intestine - dryness of the colon
E207. Large intestine - Yang deficiency (cold)
E208. Heart - Blood insufficiency
E209. Heart - Blood stagnation
E210. Heart - Fire
E211. Heart - Hot mucus clogs the heart pores

E212. Heart - Cold mucus clogs the heart pores
E213. Heart - Qi deficiency
E214. Heart - Yang deficiency
E215. Heart - Yin deficiency
E216. Liver - Ascending Liver Yang
E217. Liver - Blood deficiency
E218. Liver - Blood stagnation
E219. Liver - Moisture heat in liver and gall bladder
E220. Liver - Fire
E221. Liver - Gall bladder Qi-Empty
E222. Liver - Cold in the liver meridian
E223. Liver - Qi stagnation
E224. Liver - Wind
E225. Liver - Wind with ascending liver Yang
E226. Liver - Wind with blood anemic
E227. Liver - Wind with extreme heat
E228. Lung - Qi deficiency
E229. Lung - Mucus-moisture in the lungs
E230. Lung - Mucus-heat in the lungs
E231. Lung - Mucus-cold in the lungs
E232. Lung - Dryness of the lungs
E233. Lung - Wind-heat attacks the lungs
E234. Lung - Wind-cold affects the lungs
E235. Lung - Yin deficiency
E236. Stomach - Bloodstagnation
E237. Stomach - Fire
E238. Stomach - Cold with liquid
E239. Stomach - Nutrition stagnation
E240. Stomach - Qi deficiency
E241. Stomach - Rebellious Qi
E242. Stomach - Yin Emptiness
E243. Spleen - Heat and moisture attack the spleen
E244. Spleen - Coldness and moisture affects the spleen
E245. Spleen - Qi deficiency
E246. Spleen - Qi deficiency + Declining spleen Qi
E247. Spleen - Qi deficiency + spleen does not control the blood
E248. Spleen - Yang deficiency
E249. Kidney - Heart and kidney no longer communicate
E250. Kidney - Jing deficiency
E251. Kidney - Kidneys cannot receive the Qi
E252. Kidney - Qi is not stable
E253. Kidney - Yang deficiency
E254. Kidney - Yin deficiency

For further information visit di-book.com.